Luke Beesley | New Works on Paper

New Poems

GIRAMONDO POETS

Luke Beesley | New Works on Paper

First published 2013
from the Writing & Society Research Centre
at the University of Western Sydney
by the Giramondo Publishing Company
PO Box 752 Artarmon NSW 1570 Australia
www.giramondopublishing.com

Designed by Harry Williamson
Typeset by Andrew Davies
in 10/16.5 pt Baskerville

Printed and bound by Ligare
Distributed in Australia by NewSouth Books

National Library of Australia
Cataloguing-in-Publication data:

Beesley, Luke.
New Works on Paper.
ISBN 9781922146403 (pbk)
A821.4

Zoë and Ari

Other books by Luke Beesley

Lemon Shark
Balance

Leaves around the door are pencilled losses
John Ashbery

Say wood *and everything is clean again*
Kevin Hart

Contents

the word

(Otways)

House

bees are like charcoal
only a hint of yellow to them
I have been staring at the fire like it was a television
eventually everything is

By Wrote (Two Attempts)

after Virginia Woolf's 'In The Orchard', 1923

thin violet sunlight stretched between a distant tree
and a following wren

warm breeze coming in from ocean,
a trail of static-ish rain hushed and almost

invisibly softening the view
there are few ways to begin a poem carefully

violently the sun suffocating the limb of a tree
when the following day

I walked out on the green lawn, and looked closer
at the warm bark, I had a notion of slicing the twig-

tail and cleaning my teeth with it (as
they do in parts of Northern India)

but this is only a poem
a picked up op-shop guitar, untuned

when the bark left the tree, and if
the bath was empty, I would – wet and dripping

along the kitchen like the sun through
eight points of the louvre – write it

What A Pencil Can Do

Is nothing a word is unable. To undo a twisted knot, holding a fridge
to the truck, I begin drawing. I draw for two hours. You might
understand from elementary maths – or the wild oddity of a softball
in the hand compared to a tennis ball – that patterns are solved
by our bodies. (I can sleep through the night beside my lover our
bodies so thin in the same place they forget to discern – Picasso
was never patient with a pencil. Her Bonnard body beside me.)
If you unable a word from itself it becomes a sword. If you unable
a word from its shelf – feminine and utterly herself – it moves un-
noticed in her mouth. When unable to wake we have to bite each
other, or *bit* appeared at the end of sharpening. The thud. A through-
light from the blinds. Blind. A pencil is utterly blind. Is what it can do.

On Birds

I notice the varied folds of scribbled feather-work, and go over to chop wood the same colour as it. We just need a topic is what I think. Birds are endless engagements. Nothing idle about them – gloves of tension in communication, substance, meteorology, cute – contemporary art is stuffed with them, even trendy. They stink like the inside of a damp jacket they go – they are sleeves. Orange. Original in the sky. Quite stupid when confused.

In Nature

all is as all as, is yet or as yet
Gertrude Stein

Funny, to be *in* nature might be like

what? It is surprisingly icy, the sky.
Is it something within, or without?

I see as much from a window, hear.

I collect twigs. Fantastic. It's a word
I've been meaning to use it
won't take
isn't necessary, or this evening – sky.

Near is nature might be like. As in it is.

On Five

the time
it takes to retrieve kindling from the yard
takes like the word ubiquitous

easy, tapping them up like listening to
jazz with the index finger
on an oak table

sap – Japanese rice paper on
I write this down
eat it like the fire will

if asked what knows hours
what time it is
I say *fire*

Six New Works

Echoes travelling/ Off from the centre like horses
Sylvia Plath

I was hacking into firewood: common farm birds – pipits, quails and song-birds. They fold away from the axe like synchronised swimmers. This poem goes for as long as liquid takes to hit kitchen slate. Two, the scissors, one (or better) a chrysanthemum. Again, the firewood as carefully-laid birds, parcels, brown paper wrapping that held new clothes. This is the fourth poem for this page: allegations, legal documentation, a cufflink stuck in the throat – new bible. Say denouement. *Denouement.*

pencilled losses

(Northcote, Jan–May)

Peregrine Falcon

On the harbour library-green lamps swayed, and he let out a
long breath. Hoop. She would say *redolent* like cutting toast.
We stripped her. The vowel slightly raised voice as the *e* follow-
ed and pushed, gathered by a breeze, lulled briefly by a fly,
a flyscreen, or a trampoline. At Pellegrini's I reached up to
my own reflection and traced two ear infections. *Ciao* said the
waitress, arriving.

Timber Hitch

She folds over into the sunlight and I decide to use it. *Sun, light*, a study of buildings. Study of sunlight intercepting a hessian bag of oats the shade drawn, drawing. I tell her to draw a bath and laugh. She points it out – cards hearts. She calls me back on the landline and I imagine her in a paddock. The centre of the woods the tree *splintered*. Leaves the door pencilled losses (ash). It is a still life. A still life.

Light in Anne Carson

I can't eat rosemary the South Sudanese boy had a thorn embedded in his shin for more than a year before light surgery, an opening line by Anne Carson. Wound light or wounded light from a choppy bay – afternoon. It has been some time. She talked of a slipped disc or simply *back pain* reaching round to the small of her waist I thought pain was finite. Drinking water/thirsty iridescent elk in the boot of a Jaguar.

The Jaguar

After taking pencil shavings (green) out of the sharper than the air. Sharper. We put our hands on flags or flags put their sails on cough. We have each other medicine. Mine a piss-coloured lozenge yours somewhere in your mouth opened up – was about to sing melancholy Johnny Cash. We were at the ticket counter. Ordered two tickets. They were pieces of paper so we crossed the road. Passed a Jaguar after that I shaved and surprised bees calling the keeper to the sign – *removal of bees.* Half a beard! I said, as the biro leaked into the ocean swam the dugong elderly in swimsuits hot water bottle thick!

Bees Nudge the Mouth of a Feathered Rose

Handing my friend a new book of poems there is an object at
the centre of beauty, too. The tomatoes are the same colour as
her scarf – neckerchief. The violence around the neck in cinema.
The red in gun timber. Making a bowl to crush herbs in, keep oil,
a door open. Hold old change. If we fall in what's called *love* can
we what's called *matriculate* into invisibility? It's not about bees. .
There are no bees. Just delicious honey, a table, vowels sizzling
like warmed oil sliding through changes in the seasoning.

Manet, Modigliani, Monet...

I stared into the terrain of the table for a good four minutes the radio blew. Dry leaves tumbled off the fridge and I imagined these, the leaves, were the last words. There had been an interview set up with an ex-novelist, her only novel sensational – explicit sexual content – and eventually censored. As she talked to the compere the swirls of colour in a Rembrandt, the order and civilisation in the theory of a Modern, or Mondrian's earlier formless paintings which I cannot imagine, when he must have been asleep or day-dreaming the rest of the day through a straw. (And like *that* shade it was *there* when I put it to memory, and closed my eyes and placed both these – the putting and the closing – through the metaphor of a table drawer.)

Life Drawing

The day *is* pale, peeling the morning from it. No sleep again a walnut came from my ear spinning on the kitchen table the cereal. Made up, the house folds itself around a stop sign. Slow. Fast kids with blood knives, the table, and a pale still melon in the Bronwyn Lea poem – yellow. I lift it (Zoë's story: a bridge and a calf) and I stop her there, *wait*...All we leave on the world are children's names.

Loss

I can say during the sixth week I covered a fire with loose soil. A cat had killed in the yard. A bonfire from a party. And underneath the apple tree, you can read with a pizza. There is a curlew caught in curled rain guttering and its filigree way towards dying. Shades of bark against white cirrus cloud. I unhook it. A poem. I read the private pain of honeycomb or honeycombed as a verb. It lifted me. Ordinary cliff breeze. The sport section – a snapped ankle found in a column. Ink on the inside of my thumb.

Phil Took Flute

He took *flute* out of the sentence and there was an afterimage. *He took flute out of the sentence.* Breaking off a heel of bread the words crumble when you piece them back or guess. Glass had to admit to his conductor he was hearing on the limits of himself – the note could have been a C, C# – he didn't know, and welcomed help. He simply looked out of the sentence. What he saw were waves. An *impress* he thought the flute had left. Or – better – the impression the word *flute* left as they came in, went out, and he kept looking see the music hear the image over and over. I waited. Looked at my hands.

Parachutes Tumble like Confetti

There were sparrows stuck on a fence-line in the corner of a sketch. It was a lane-way in Balthus disappearing between her legs and onward past a pastry shop to the edge of the canvas – expensive nail polish long thin fingers a milky wrist. She put the catalogue down. We'd been arguing (the glue of the spine coming away – glue of *argue* coming away to a single feather). In the painting an Alsatian argued with a postman.

AI Bakery

Assembled incidents – no sadness. Nothing as obvious. The noun
collection. A collection of poems (grief) the clipped organisation
in the word and, working to define it, I sit down. The television
is reflected in the capsicum. A table over, a woman blushes opposite
her sister. Unmistakable.

A Description

It would be called *rust* somewhere in a novel. Or in a poem *sunlight caught in it*. Thin hair of her pale stomach, upper thigh. It is thinking he desires in his hands with a pencil, water crackers. A tinge in creek water below dragon-flies and leaves, knocked by light. Hears the deep

bone of her hips crack.

Diving Into a Tilted Swimming Pool

All sky-blue and useless to passing shoppers spilling on our feet
like dipping your feet in the sea last year, a leap year characterised
by storms and dandruff. Tipping pools until classes fall and Floaties
like bloated bees take flight and you feel good for the first time in a
month. Before sex in the middle of a film under the drug of a dream.
Where consequence begins messy swims and gentle flooding followed
by Christmas. A sudden relief. I set my door open using a potted
agapanthus. You prop yours using a book of African savannah animals.
You wear your aubergine swimmers that answer to no one. I peel you.

A Sign

When I met you at the lights you were holding your bike and holding your brother and your anger. Your breath clawed pedestrians. *They* you said, and it was in your mouth, the word, like sourdough bread. They! You caught the asparagus-green, oiled and wok-fried lights and began moving across the traffic like a flock of geese. Your brother called. He had been in the army – there were complicated telephones, twelve digits. He was an engineer and his nose had been broken by a bath tile. It was *you* who picked it up, too. Caught in your eye like a coin at the bottom of a public pool, a lost watch in a fling, snorkelling, sun glinting off a buckle. On the road was a sign.

Quick Warm Sunlight

Graffiti tangled on the sign, a man with saxophone breath
where Johnston St and Princes ten minute solo. Two people left.
The vocalist was nervous her lyrics she packed in a clarinet case
somehow embedded in the lining. On the corner of Smith and
Alexandra. He was telling me. His epic walk from outer suburbs.
It was hot. The sun was brassy slapping the side of my face saying
listless in beauty and how we come here rhythm only friend. Placing
a hand on my t-shirt laughed like a coin, leaving the street, singing
you and me between – we need. And with the sweet need only…

Primary Colours

A woman on her back tangled in the shade of a tree, and further down towards the gully three men leapt at the same time shouting *it's over, it's over*. My yoga instructor was overweight. Fixed-gear cyclists *wished* on the slope behind me. A man dressed in black – adhesive shade? – walked by with a yellow zucchini in his hand. Listening to early Nigerian jazz. The way he smiled so young around the museum a balcony of primary colours. I drank up. Yoghurt drink. Added my fingernail to the acres of Carlton Gardens.

The Mugger With Immaculate Facial Hair

Dirt with kids in it. Flaking paint. Clouds the shape of scars. Sex on a tile on her knee over Christmas in her cousin's basement apartment. The mugger at a popular concert. Easy essay. Chest of drawers. The clothes we ate with tomato sauce. In an aircraft hanger two coats one made of wool the other made of wheels. Buttons. Expensive jackets. Mercedes on the end of her neck – hospital for weeks. The hospital that broke her or the break that made it to the hospital. Pig jitters (nervous whores, 19th Century, guns in their pants, pillows.) Timber that floats before exploding. Marriages drenched by tide or protest. Lovely printmakers' hands. Metal folds the memory before idea.

Small Talk

The solicitor asked me *so what do you write about?* He had gotten someone off, and filed the *necessary papers* – a neat fax making its way. I didn't know what to say. There was a frustrated tone to his voice as if he hadn't found anything in tragedy. *Tragedy* I said why not? Put a sentence to memory with my wheel-barrow, sweated in forty-three degree heat. Woke up with a virus. After curry. Saw my grandmother's anti-depressants on the radio with dixieland-swing lessons. I could feel his jaw against my knuckles but I thought of Gandhi. I opened a sachet of pepper and he sneezed. Spaghetti arrived to complement the wine and my hand went to my wife's (I'm not married) napkin to stop it
falling. Busty waitress.

Oranges

Walking away from a pile of oranges the sunset spills to the corner of a blanket. We must have a setting! Two chairs a table Danish cutlery a note of remorse. A lamp tipped to offer sacrifice my little cousin hit kid with his knuckles leaving his chest like a budgerigar lost to the trees which later formed a bruise and found itself tattooed with the caption *we are free*. It's been a month since decisions. *Decisions* like rubbing cinnamon on your biceps before the physiotherapist.

Movies

De Niro sights a rare deer through spidery glass and pumps the Winchester – shocks the buck into an awkward stopped posture, twitching. Whether on film or thinking I'm pushed into my seat as in take-off. *Parliamentarians* I think this word out with chipped timber – logging – because I'm reminded I'm reading a newspaper. It folds over my arms like the wounded, electrocuted child in the orange parka in poor, beautiful weather – Connecticut – in Ang Lee's *The Ice Storm*.

Serena Williams' Earring Fell

Serena's earring fell off during a point. A linesman gasped. The crowd shushed him. I kept the crowd's sound with me, and pinned it to the trajectory of the jewellery. We could have disappeared (disappeared into thought, I thought, turning a coin over). Thick shade touching the inside of her ear was a part, a point itself.

Olivia popped round and sat down and we talked about the players' clothes. I didn't know whether to leave it on. Serena was up, and would no doubt finish off the match. We talked some more and I looked at Olivia's hands and she asked me, in all seriousness, for I knew she didn't care for sport, generally – *What's a point?*

Lucian Freud Keats

Here, Tuesday, are the lips of Lucian Freud's subjects. Just expelled breath. Despairing, disinterested breath. Real! Peppery day. Outside the library gusts of up to 150 km/h. Dour or nifty elderly women. Red freckles. Tasmania. Tuesday with a handful of rock shavings the colour of steak. You have your leg on my knee. I ask *how* and you reply *like a spinning speed boat*. Or *sweat scraped from a racehorse*.

Pronouncing Barthelme

I'm about to describe my method. I'll never get past it – the resemblance of bread to the word *description*. Jesus dinner. Method in the flour. Flour in the hair. Start like a haircut or an ant bite. Green and brown hair black snake. Or find description anywhere. Cereal. The back of a novel – *Clean as pebbles* (the prose). Tasty dessert basically on the same page. That's it. Find two pages of description and pitch a two-man tent. Call fire trucks, two police and a charity. Open your books – all the ones you bought. Crouch by biscuits with your arm over your neighbour's yard. Prepare tea without using your mind. I was using my mind. If you get arrested by the turquoise ricochet off the face of your watch – see. Time everything down to the last comma. Hiss.

frames

This is a Poem Without Mothers

The alarm in the morning is made of rubber
invents the day around it like a drum. Leonard Cohen.

Um. The alarm in the morning is made of stones
we unearthed near a horse. My father, smoking a cigar.

The drip in the tap is the colour of moss. It drips five.
Six. Again, I taste rust wake nicotine – my grandfather.

A faucet, digital alarm clock, green, ripe olive
porcelain awakening. Rare fish skit, arc. Robert Hass.

This is a poem without mothers.

Two Star Recollections with David Cronenberg

ii.

Meanwhile Freud's beard was a brook. Trout swam out of his cigar. Sunlight caught through the smoke and illuminated silver whiskers. He spoke slowly. Each thought was a smoke ring on its path disintegrating on the edge of a table, or the bowed back support of a teak sitting chair. Halos falling out of his face – dismissed in his papers, disgusted in Jung...

iii.

I do remember Lucerne's dying lion, and the newly renovated timber footbridge – eaten by a fire (tossed cigarette). I walked over it
circa 1997/1998?

i.

In the new terrible film of Jung and Freud, Jung is sitting in his
dining room.
I can see out the window just behind his ear, greenery sloping to a lake. Had I been to Zurich? I had an inkling that only a touch, a slight press of concentration, would give me an answer. Instead I watched Keira Knightly's jaw jut forward beneath humiliation (her word) and in time I knew I had not. Basel and Lucerne, even Geneva, but never Zurich.

Twelve Parts Portrait Philip Glass

documentary film, Scott Hicks

We walk across the road moving on to the music Glass asks a question and the answer is bread/hair/bread/mouse the bakery is symmetrical in the distance, and the bread's perfume tangles in plane trees filled with sparrows. What they make of this only scientists beginning a new page of research – the tables and slipstreams, the dirty little birds getting into half-eaten ideas, tossed clarinet solos...

We keep on, close to the park, careful as the ego goes settling in the poplar branches, then springing again to hover above a mouse or rabbit, urban fox, even, late in the day. He rode his bicycle to the studio until the studio itself was a bicycle. The bicycle of the studio. Twin Studios, as it became, was a rhyme with wheel that needed fixing and he retuned to the studio daily sheet music – sharpener, utensils – to inspect the twirl and balance, could draw out his music while riding to the studio until the studio itself was a bicycle. The bicycle yellow weathered and smelling of old mattress worn in the shape of its rider, hunched and curled into his own (stage three) sleep. His four-year-old son dropping drinking glasses on the step and then throwing them into the grass. The scene as he goes outside, begins picking it up out of the lawn and Glass moving around in his fingers his wife's distrait and fatigue and the opera unknown to them all now pencilled into every possible step and walk toward the ocean.

Sea Things (26 Poems)

Not Much is Known About How Fish Sleep

Like broken bread the ship fell away –
squid, kelp, carbon

Car bonnet

(The sea also has carbon in it)

I was lifting a film of carbon

Copy paper from a receipt book

When I went into the water my hands forward
towards the wave

Two thoughts – like solicitors leaving separate offices – one

Around the inlet at the base of your neck
two the word *estuary*

Fish move like litter

Glitter

In Robert Hass' recent collection

Time and Materials

He uses it three times to describe
light on sea water

'and glittering sea', 'glittering sea' and
'the water glitters hard against it'

Thursday – daylight in it
Unusually large day and the stories of hearsay and lunacy
on the sea.

Through history crime happened on a Thursday, as did
ecstasy. Take a whale. Lay it on a picnic blanket.

The Clicking Sound of a Reef When You Put Your Head Into the Sea

Yesterday's Thursday poem. I didn't know it at the time

It was Wednesday

Sometimes the day tricks you and you allow it
like salmon at the other table, a muscle –
the calf – that aches after swimming.
The sea is like the skin of lettuce today. Is room temperature.
I open a drawer. Beside my bed filling up
all night the sea moves below me like
Christmas.

The Sea in the 1980s

On holidays
I went to the sea and was lifted out of it by my father
who was looking elsewhere   a wave

Folded pieces of paper

In the 80s the sea was bluer owing to northern light
skipping off the pawpaw-coloured swimsuits and
something to do with tide and starlight, washed atmosphere,
a broken-up comet.
I don't know. In the 80s the sea was bluer
I was about eleven
It came up to my shoulders

Attempt To Get Oats Into This Poem

for Bishop Druitt College

It was no reflection on my fondness for you, the throwing of the sour milk. The sound of the silver bucket spread out like a town at the beginning of a Kurosawa. The milk was: *hula*. The day: *ultra marine*. You stepped in the mood. Do you still follow bees? I found four in a tea pot...

On the cover of your book is an open locket and within it your relatives? Cousins? Their faces are small but I can recognise your eyes. With what poems will you describe them this Christmas? *Christmas* like the name Tony Tuckson. I guess, I see spilled paint across the canvas like a pulled muscle.

We could get a towel, or sit in the sun? There's a bus! And our reflection in it, turning. It was my thought today that as poets we should eat good breakfasts. You? Oats, sliced pear, pepitas, other seeds, natural yogurt.

Influence

I'd like to have your address so that I can break into your house and steal something. I want to squeeze between the rose bush and trestle above your front gate so as not to disturb your work or sleep and lift the gate latch carefully and lay it down again. I imagine you sensitive to the sounds of your surrounds. I could move without shoes and in pools of darkness provided by leaf foliage, to avoid the moon.

There will be a path down one side of your house and I will follow it with my hands because I believe I can imagine architecture. It will be close to the neighbour's fence and he won't have a dog. I will crouch in the true posture of a thief with my hands forward and my dark clothes.

I read somewhere that when you write you like to close the blinds and write near a blank wall, without wall hangings. I have no interest in your art collection but I am nearing the corner of your life.

When I have your address in my hands I will put it to memory and then fold it numerously and swallow it at the corner of your house where there is one single purple flower. You will have a screen door or a French door. It's where I am with a small screwdriver or a piece of plastic removed from the collar of a business shirt. Can you give me your address in a small inner-city terrace house? Or a detached terrace with a small garden in the front and, as I've mentioned, along the side of the house a small breeze where the lilac swayed like a musician. Or a train. 'Celerity Breeze' could be the name of jazz leaking from your wireless near which I take a watch that sits like a two-legged spider. I put it on and go to your study where I wear the watch that you left there, too.

I have an image of you, also, pulling shiny molasses-black records from their sleeves, bringing the records close to your mouth, and blowing the dust away in one quick breath. Later when asleep you hear the quiet distant thunder. Though it's not the quiet distant thunder at all but the full-length mirror which disguises a cupboard in your spare room and I am opening it very slowly. One sheet of lightning. Another pool coming away in my hands like a fish in the moonlight. Hidden. Not an affair, again, not an affair. Nor a jewel or your wife but a path – I take your time.

Murray Bail's The Pages

Murray Bail's comparison of two
chairs in his novel *the pages*. A *table* chair
lame as a donkey, *deck-*
brown as vintage tea strainers. Anticipation
of messages is as distracting as doing four or
five things at once, sickening a task (ABC
Radio National, June, morning).
Murray Bail's *the pages* three
points of humour. Narration.
A man sits down to a coffee
in Sydney. In Sydney a man
sits to the sound of a Bondi
wave unwrapped and discard-

ed on the pavement. Sydney
is always in the 1940s, and is very young, yet
so very old. The apprehension. Pages
tucked through a button hole you heard your
stomach and a car door shut
expensively – intestinal hiccup.

Melancholy

for year 8 Peninsular School

I went to the races but the races were slow
I forgot to eat
I was thin and near a lake
I had to look for a *phrase* on the tree
I spent some time deciding wintermelon
Or watermelon
(I could find no rockmelon)
I could feel my brain working it out like cooking sausages
Eventually I was able to make a small fire and a hot dog
It was a good bun
Like insulation we put in our house no more than a day ago
I was on the roof
The suburb was busy
My neighbour pulled a cauliflower out of the earth and started
eating it
My neighbour was rude.
I fell off the roof or just got down and went inside and looked in
the crisper
I looked in the crisper
In the crisper
The word *Antarctica*

Office

Going to and leaving scuffed planets, she drove her nail across a cake of soap. Waves peeled off Bondi. Cafés continued in fine, hip disinterest. She scrubbed the table, then, and fell into hot traffic. It was a kind of legalised man slaughter: the archaic, better rested, individual, circumstantial, ontological, piecemeal (we were drowning between surf lifesavers, flags primary colours. Used car sales. To think, the kids swum up through the passenger-side window. Both had moustaches. Salesmen quick phrases slugs squeezed out of envelopes soft packs and packages stitched canvas or cotton from India, Pakistan, Bangladesh, waxy blood-coloured signatures stitching books with dental floss.) Her teeth were smashed! Getting up, she swore bloody at cars and limped to the corner store and ordered two ice-creams...

Sydney staged a fight/stayed one night sun cream pale arms and the power of injunction, punctuation, apostrophe. It was an apostrophe! A secular ecstasy on the sand! A round fat cut glistened on her elbow though this was pantomime, a port of inconsistent sailor jokes. Blue jokes in overalls and the blue bay in the mouth of a strangled burglar. (Thieves know the tip-toe and the train line, the blue-grey rock the blue shadow.) To dress in hot disguise with a clean white house in a blue-black suit pocket of business cards islands off the coast of corn-coloured light over lawn from oblong windows. Houses ocean liners dogs slept all next day boats putter argyle strides emerge with nine irons zippers up smirks and milking demonstration in men's shoes – steak dragging great clouds of fragrance out back into George like muddy explorers. Elderly, their arms wrinkled as udders, outraged and chatting politely to high-school kids in grape or pea-green uniforms. Sydney – so very young, so very old – newly discovered planet. How do we get our head around it? The heavy high watermark of the harbour celebrity residence coordination in Glebe book binding us here and there a foot facial relapse three days each morning in a pair of Reeboks laces so long it takes a half hour to trace my way to the universe and maths of chance time and let's, oysters.

Figures in Frame

I have always hoped, in a sense, to be able to paint the mouth
like Monet painted a sunset. But I have never succeeded...

Sister Mercedes described Bacon's heart attack as tremendous – see?
Repeated coughing, the filigree tightness of breathing, a chest

of drawers, the leather stale air of a discarded piano accordion,
steep stairs leading up to his studio from coach stables.

Bacon designed furniture for years in the 1950s
and was tutored in Paris, perhaps? The tiered

desk he pencilled was noticed as an Adam's apple in
1952 whilst drinking and physical sexual contact.

Tremendous said the nun with cunning and detachment
– innocence – wedded to the chest, to the father with a capital f...

Bacon's favourite letter they said in lower case across art books
he dared not appreciate

in his late 70s the Velasquez, finally. You see him over
in the corner of the gallery his hands in his ears

pockets pricked
lonely. Unhappy.

↙

Waking in this
strange house
my cheek is wet.

Blood? Rising I turn
a light on – saliva,
a dream about asthma.

The Sun is Green Over the Lawn

The sun is green
through that drink, juice is it?
Guava. The sun is green on her chin. The green
sun of night-time. The green light inside
a canary. The lake you ate. Lettuce in the spring. A long lettuce. The
green men of Atwood's poems. The nasty
sleep. Light before the storm. Her
green bath. Stepping in a green bath. Matisse's
Japanese lover's green
cheeks.

Hem of a Shuttlecock

after Ern Malley's 'Sybilline'

The coat of yours with strawberries at the heart pocket, clotted
stitches at its upper collar, is the poem. Ampersand was too clever,
as were your sleeves which admit heritage door knobs sliced off
and sold in Old Delhi markets or snuck into Sotheby's...
I found your letter in a dish cloth. Ships.
Ships as in blue-vein cheese blue and swirling font. Funny place
to discover it. I expected the dentist, now – his nostrils and peculiar
binoculars his magnified glimpses twitched (biting the poor man's
hand). Afterwards, clean and smiling at the dog bark, spits of
rain, a corduroy wallet, and the driver's-side airbag (in sequence,
a quick bloom). We turned left into Conaught Place her hand-
writing was nonsense (!) taller than a dessert spoon and angled
fiercely north north east firm breeze and the already laboured
attempt at what's the verb for unique unique the horizon I always
side with (neglect concept) trust the deep recess of the quick
sprinkle, thought. In no time it was slack-neck midday. You were
asleep on the deck, depressed. Clinical silence drowned out the
blood beat in the head. And with this – a clear, clean, tooth-
white quiet – I began a reply. Dear pet, dear trauma, we moved
off course the ocean is expressionless in the mirror I toilet my
face with creams juice cereal we are living in one neat breath!

Let it breathe. We sit the journey out to let it breathe! Washed
up discovering a response falling out of a bowl like a five-dollar
note grey as a porpoise swimming up each phase of your shiver

slash haemorrhage at the collar. I don't even know if we exist or what? Have fallen off? The back of a deck of cards? Discarded. Heartless. The opening scene in Scorcese's *King of Comedy* – Jerry Lewis' indifference to meaning/comfort. A Beaufort familiar hush (shoe) shuffle. Your Victorian accoutrements. Hem of a shuttlecock.

Red Lines Horizontal, Flat White or Number Six Seed Cycle for Cy

Cut a painting up and let them be lost to the wind
Yoko Ono 'Piece for the Wind'

i. Terrible Coffee

ran over like a dirty beach. I tried to evoke impressionism &
received a seated, outboard motor of an ovation. I had aged. Henri
Matisse stop lights, or, closer, salmon over the Twombly of my nose. Sip. There
was a cup of disrespect in her eyes, pay issues. This *deja vu*. At the 3/4 mark
acid-free paper and swiftly, for I know not of trams sliding down Burke St like
oysters, small islands toasted off noted criticism, coded, sentimental...
took three men to roll a small *r* into the bed of a truck. Europe waited
all day/sleeping in/getting up to Liszt in D

ii. Flat

aggrandising – grandstanding iodine's half-life assistant pigment stale Robert Motherwell or spilled, botched muscle in a business shirt netball skirt pom-pom ruffle. Skip of stones lost medicine. Picked up a year later by lemonade sales on love's tendency. Actually, a lost word. Tense! In the past, her shoes worn only on Fridays washed on Sundays outside on the lawn regular shampoo expensive polish polish them the money rises – economy index quiver verb slip crash etc etiquette requiring coffee cough (alkaline) weather trough ease-ing on the pavement c/o Murray-line hygiene & gonzo

iii. Beat

enjambment. What's the time? It's tomorrow! She said this exiting a theatre:
two washed-up actors abseil their faces into script edits & promo junkets.
We suppose Jakarta. Twenty-one-year-old lemonade flat as a cummerbund or,
better, shadow boxer feeling the night, linoleum in it...

iv. Orange Swear

quarter moon trigger for it. Power. Sooty-thin gun cloud a whisper
into her neck. A few grams of breath-like climate, in situ. The clock arm
moves like a pony tail. We bring coincidence to roasted shadow in figure
eights, thrown down with *pinot noir*. I feel utterly grey (white with a little purple
in it). A mole on her inner thigh. Turning a page to enter intercourse, that gentle
twist of the pepper shaker, I hear her shoulder reconstruction like the gravel-
ly nibs in wild flowers

v. Cursive

gulls splash flocks of cloud obliterated & oblivious as coffee froth.
Stray plankton on her ear lobe & pinching it off I inspect her hair
for nits. She itches the back of her knee where a finch stretches & collapses.
Smooth in the palm I make a door knob. A cliff, littered in spittle,
& busy shop condiments a used appliance. Nits are, considerably,
in her hair – punctuation nestled in her part, her bone-white
scalp like a tablecloth in Dürer, Cézanne

vi. Still

unspecific yellow bird on a limb of greenery, lost in the needle-
eye of a cursive *e*. Myth on her hip and a choked breeze unnamed –
dragging desert-beige, clotted heart-attack cheese – across a table. Hands
move like wrens probably robins sewing up a point or tone, ruffled.
It's as if our own desire to possess the language of music – if for a lean year,
or an unknown dog – by chance directs us

Notes

The book's epigraphs come from John Ashbery's poem, 'Meaningful Love', from his collection *Where Shall I Wander* (2005); and Kevin Hart's poem, 'The Word', from his Giramondo book *Young Rain* (2008). '*Quick warm sunlight* came running from Berkeley road, swiftly, in slim sandals, along the brightening footpath.', is my favourite sentence in Joyce's *Ulysses* (1922). The title 'The Clicking Sound of a Reef When you Put Your Head into the Sea', is a line from the Michael Ondaatje poem, 'Sweet Like A Crow', from his collection, *There's a Trick With a Knife I'm Learning to Do: Poems 1963-1978* (1979). Italicised lines in the poem, 'Glitter', come from Robert Hass' collection, *Time and Materials: Poems 1997-2005* (2007). The poem, 'Twelve Parts Portrait Philip Glass', sits alongside Scott Hicks' documentary *Portrait of Philip Glass in Twelve Parts* (2008). Incidentally, the title, 'Phil took Flute', comes from a conversation between the filmmaker and Glass' sister, Sheppie Abramowitz, about Glass' school days. The poem, 'Murray Bail's *The Pages*', makes reference to Bail's 2008 novel of that name. 'Two Star Recollections with David Cronenberg', of course, refers to his 2011 film, *A Dangerous Method*. The poems in 'Pencilled Losses' mark a return to composing the first draft of my poems in pencil.

Acknowledgements

Poems in *New Works on Paper* have been published in *Australian Poetry Journal, The Age, The Australian Literary Review, Best Australian Poems 2010, Best Australian Poems 2012, Blue Dog, Cordite, The Disappearing, Island, FourW, Overland, Rabbit Poetry Journal, Readings' 'Poetry for the People' Series, Red Room Company Papercuts Anthology 2011, Red Room Company* (online), *Southerly* and *Westerly,* with thanks to the editors. In 2010, *ABC Radio National's* 'Poetica' broadcast 'The Clicking Sound of a Reef When You Put Your Head Into The Sea', and, 'Yesterday and Day Length', from 'Sea Things (26 Poems)', a sequence commissioned by Red Room Company. Grateful acknowledgement to Arts Victoria for a grant to complete poems in the 'Pencilled Losses' section. These poems were edited in a writers' studio at the former Boyd residence, Glenfern, thanks to the Victorian Writers Centre. Some 'Pencilled Losses' poems appeared in the catalogue of my solo exhibition of drawings, *Authors* (2011). The poems 'Melancholy' and 'Attempt to Get Oats Into this Poem' were commissioned by Red Room Company for their *Papercuts* poets-in-schools project. The sequence 'Red Lines Horizontal...' was completed with the assistance of a State Library of Victoria Creative Fellowship (2010/11). The poem, 'The Sun is Green Over the Lawn', appeared with a different title and form in the chapbook *Balance* (2012), published by Whitmore Press. For *Cordite*, the poems 'This is Poem About Mothers', and 'The Sign', were translated into Korean (2011), and the poem, 'Timber Hitch', was translated into Bahasa Indonesian (2012). The poem, 'Six New Works', appeared in the exhibition, 'Addition and Erasure', at Margaret Lawrence Gallery (2010). Thank you, also, to Zoë Miller, Nicholas Powell, Bonny Cassidy & Tim Grey (and their Melbourne poetry workshops), Kate Middleton, Nathan Shepherdson and Michael Farrell. And particular thanks to the editors, Alice Grundy and Fiona Wright, and to Ivor Indyk.

This project has been assisted by the Victorian Government through the Arts Victoria Developing Writers' Program and by the Commonwealth Government through the Australia Council, its arts funding and advisory body.